So, Do You Want a Job, or What?

So, Do You Want a Job, or What?

Dirty Secrets of Resume Writing and Job Hunting

John L. Nicodemus

The Silloway Press
Columbia, MD

So, Do You Want a Job, or What?
Dirty Secrets of Resume Writing and Job Hunting

Copyright 2011 John L. Nicodemus.
All rights reserved.

No part of this book may be reproduced or transmitted in any form or by any means, electronic or mechanical, including photocopying, recording, or by an information storage and retrieval system without written permission from the author, except for the use of brief quotations for inclusion in a review.

This book is published for general reference and is not intended to be a substitute for independent verification by readers when necessary and appropriate. The book is sold with the understanding that neither the author nor publisher is engaged in rendering any legal or accounting advice. Although the author and publisher have prepared the manuscript with care and diligence, and have made every effort to ensure the accuracy and completeness of the information contained within, we assume no responsibility for errors, inaccuracies, omissions, or inconsistencies.

Printed in the United States of America

LCCN: 2010943035
ISBN: 978-0-9831552-0-1

The Silloway Press, 9437 Clocktower Lane, Columbia, MD 21046
301-335-9368 – So@SillowayPress.com – http://SillowayPress.com

I would like to dedicate this book to all those individuals with whom I have worked in the employment groups in the Annapolis, Maryland area. They have taught me a lot, and assisting them in their job searches has been tremendously rewarding.

Acknowledgments

I would like to acknowledge both John Covington and Rodger Findiesen who created two of the employment groups with whom I work. John was the one who inspired me to write this book, and both John and Rodger continue to demonstrate how important both the topic and the employment groups are.

I would also like to thank my publisher, Peg Silloway, for making the entire publishing process as easy as it could possibly be.

Contents

Introduction 11

Part I
Dirty Secrets of Resume Writing

Chapter 1 – Why Write a Resume Anyway? 17

Chapter 2 – Know Your Audience 23

Chapter 3 – Common Resume Pitfalls 27

Chapter 4 – Types of Resumes 31

Part II
Dirty Secrets of Job Hunting

Chapter 5 – Organizing Your Search Campaign 39

Chapter 6 – Goal Setting and Metrics 45

Chapter 7 – Maintaining a Positive Attitude 51

Chapter 8 – Entrepreneurship and Independent Income Streams 55

Chapter 9 – Selling Yourself 61

Appendix – Sample Resume Formats 67

About the Author 73

Index 75

Introduction

I wrote this book as a way to "cut to the chase" in the job-hunting arena. There is a lot of misunderstanding out there about both resumes and effective job searches, and the more one reads about job-hunting strategies and resume formats, the more confusing things get. Now some of what is in this book you may have heard before, but never in a way that makes it so clear and so applicable TODAY to helping you find a good job in a time of extremely intense competition.

This book is written to be a quick read that zeroes in on the critical issues that most people miss. There are a number of "dirty secrets" that most books and experts do not mention. These secrets materially impact the success of any job search and need to be clearly explained. A job seeker who knows the secrets can develop effective strategies to gain an edge in today's job market. This book provides a short and concise summary of these dirty secrets and strategies to overcome them.

So what gives me the expertise to write this book you may be wondering. As an individual and business coach, I volunteered to mentor an employment group organized by a local church. In relatively short order, I found that I was mentoring three groups. That mentoring experience really hit home with me on a number of levels, the primary one being my amazement at the lack of understanding of the job-hunting process that most people have. I guess that I should not be surprised, since most people have not experienced this process as many times as I have (both as a job seeker and potential employer), and those who have experienced it have not done so in an economic slump as deep as the one the country is in now.

When I joined these mentoring groups as an expert to offer my advice on their search, that is all that I thought would happen. Lo and behold, I found myself learning as much, if not more, from those I was mentoring. I also discovered the power of a support group to those in the middle of a job search. The continuous positive reinforcement that a group offers is priceless. I would strongly encourage everyone who is involved in a job search to join a support group; if you cannot find one, start your own. It is that valuable a tool.

Two areas in which support groups can really help keep you on track is in following advice and mapping out a job search strategy. I wrote this book to provide direct and honest tips on both resumes and the process of job hunting. Since I am not a subtle or politically correct type of person, I think you will find that most of the advice is blunt and very straightforward. And while it is relatively easy to give advice, taking or following that advice is anything but. You are not alone, and in this economy, being without a job is nothing about which you should feel shame.

The big secret about the job hunting process is that you must "sell yourself." If you have never had sales training, you must read this book to gain an understanding of these new skills that strike at the core of your job search.

Introduction

As I talk about throughout the book, you will need to do lots of research on the process. If you Google the terms "job search," "accomplishment resume," and other appropriate job-hunting terms, you will find a plethora of information on the Internet. I have tried to synthesize a lot of different sources with what I have learned over the years, but I would encourage you not to take my word for it. More important, talk with others about your search and your mindset. Having a sounding board will have a positive impact on your outlook and results!

Good Luck and Good Hunting!

Part I

Dirty Secrets of Resume Writing

Chapter 1

Why Write a Resume Anyway?

Why do you need a resume? I have posed this question to many job seekers and have gotten a lot of logical, but misguided answers. In order to develop an effective resume, you truly need to understand the essential purpose of a resume. Similar to how a tool can be used for a number of purposes, a resume serves multiple ends. Just as tools can be adapted for specific jobs, a resume can be customized to address various job opportunities. A resume also has a more vital function that is almost always overlooked by both professional resume services and individuals writing their own resumes.

Let us take a look at a hammer as an example. We would all agree that the primary function of a hammer is to drive in nails, but it may also be used to pry out nails. It is used to square up boards, position objects prior to fastening them in place, lever objects into place, and a myriad of other functions, of which I (an extremely poor handyman) have not even thought up. We all know from experience that those who know the secrets of wielding a hammer can do amazing things. We also know that those of us who do not possess this knowledge and experience can do great harm with the same tool. How many of us have ever missed the target and hit our thumbs or inadvertently put a hole in the wall while trying to hang a picture?

Now let us take this analogy and apply it to resumes. Many people have told me that they wrote a resume to get a job. Sorry, but you just whacked your thumb with that hammer! **A resume will not get you a job** (our first dirty secret)! Let me say that again: A resume will not get you a job. What a resume can do is get you an interview. Once you have the interview, your personality and interviewing skills must carry you the rest of the way. The reverse, however, is true: A resume can cost you a job. If you lie or significantly distort the truth on your resume, you can lose a job that you have been offered or even accepted.

Many respondents have also told me that a resume communicates their experience and work history. If you believe that, you have hit the nail a glancing blow and bent it. Yes, a resume does communicate those things, but if that is all you are trying to communicate with your resume, you will find the job search road a long and winding one. I hope you are starting to see that you need to understand the true purposes of a resume in order to gain the full benefit from the process and write one that gets your foot in the door for that all-important interview.

So what is a resume's true purpose? I define a resume as *a tool that clearly and effectively communicates your accomplishments, skills, employment, and educational background to others.*

The most important use of a resume, in my opinion, is implied in the above definition. In order for a resume to "clearly and effectively communicate," it must be focused. In order for you to write a focused resume, you must stop and take the time to **understand and appreciate what**

Why Write a Resume Anyway?

you bring to the table in a potential employment situation (our next secret), which is not necessarily an easy task. You are bringing skills and knowledge (and that is all that most people include in their resumes), but you are also bringing drive, ambition, enthusiasm, diligence, leadership, and a host of other intangibles, all of which are the very attributes upon which most hiring decisions are made. To be successful in an interview, you must be able to talk (as opposed to brag) about your intangible assets. Writing an effective resume is the first step in being able to do this confidently.

Most of us tend to undervalue our attributes and overemphasize our faults. We know, in our heart of hearts, that the home run we hit at work last year was pure dumb luck. We also know that it was not us; it was our team that made it happen. With these thoughts roaming around in our heads, we tend to minimize our own impact. (In later chapters we will discuss "selling yourself" which is exactly what you are doing in a job search.) In order to sell effectively, you have to "know your product" — in other words, what you bring to the table with a potential employer. Building a good resume will allow you to clarify your thoughts on your product's benefits.

A resume is not the place for modesty; neither is it the place for puffery and bluster (this is another dirty secret). What you need is an honest and aggressive description of what you have accomplished (as opposed to what tasks your past jobs entailed). Think about it: Was that home run truly dumb luck, or was it the result of you following your gut feelings? Sure, the team got the result, but what was your role? Did you inspire the team, lead the team, or otherwise guide the team to the result (you need not have been the "team leader" to do this)? What desirable intangibles to you bring to the table? You need to answer these questions honestly. This will give you the focus and self-awareness that you want while writing your resume. In addition, it will give you the confidence to talk about your background and accomplishments in a way that will come across as sincere and honest during an interview and that will get you the job!

Homework

Women typically have more difficulty with this than men. Men readily take credit for any accomplishment, even if they had nothing to do with it. Women, however, tend to deflect credit to others, even when they should take credit. Write down 15 to 20 (or more if you can) accomplishments about which you are particularly proud. These can be things in any area of your life including church, social, or fraternal organizations; volunteer organizations and events; work; sports; or any other areas which seem appropriate. Obviously, the more work-related accomplishments, the better.

Here are some questions you can answer to help formulate your accomplishments (courtesy of Mike Peduto, Managing Partner of Stevton Consulting, who provided these tips to an employment group that I am mentoring):

- Did you identify a problem and solve it?
- Did you save the company money?
- Did you manage systems, people, or processes?
- Were you selected for awards or bonuses?
- Did you participate in decision-making?
- Of what moments are you most proud?

Why Write a Resume Anyway?

You are trying to capture not just your skills but also those intangible qualities (leadership, drive, determination, decisiveness, independent thinking, initiative, compassion, etc.) for which you think a potential employer is looking. Try to include solid measurable results wherever possible (for example, cost savings of X dollars, efficiency gains of Y percent, reduction in processing time of Y percent, increased sales of X dollars).

Once you have done that, put the document in a drawer for a few days. When you take it out and reread it, begin the editing process. This may take several editing sessions (with a day or so between sessions). Your goal is to have these accomplishments described in one or two sentences or less. Each accomplishment should begin with a strong action verb (led, developed, implemented, executed, etc.). This opening verb should be put in a bold italic font. This will give you the basic building blocks for your resume.

Chapter 2

Know Your Audience

Any writer of either fiction or non-fiction (hopefully the category with which we are dealing) will tell you that you have to know your audience to be successful. For resumes, you have a number of potential audiences. If you are responding to an advertisement, your initial audience could be an optical scanner searching for key words within the resume. Your initial audience could also be an overworked HR person who has been tasked to sort through hundreds of resumes. If you are lucky, your audience could be someone who has some say over the hiring decision, or it could be the actual decision-maker.

In spite of all the effort and work that you put into your resume, if you are responding to an advertisement, you may be only one of perhaps hundreds of applicants. One lady I spoke with was told, after asking the company about the timing of the hiring process, that she was one of 2,732 qualified applicants for the position. **In these situations, there is no chance that anyone will actually read your resume** (another dirty secret). At best, your resume will be scanned by a live human being for about 10 or 15 seconds. If you have not grabbed the reader by then, you have lost the battle.

The person reviewing these mounds of resumes is faced with the task of reducing the numbers down to a reasonable few to call in for interviews. He/she is looking for qualified candidates, and **it does not matter if the most qualified candidate does not make the cut** (dirty secret). What matters is that those who are selected for interviews are qualified to do the job. When faced with this kind of task, a reviewer will begin looking for reasons to eliminate candidates. Thus **a resume is used to eliminate prospects** (yet another dirty secret). As the resume writer, your job is twofold: (1) to make sure your resume highlights what you bring to the table on the first half of the first page, and (2) to eliminate as many possible negatives as you can.

People with lots of experience who have worked for three or more different employers over the years may reasonably have a two- or three-page resume. The chances that the initial reviewer gets to page two would be amazing. Think about what happens if you scatter critical information throughout a multi-page resume. There is a good chance that it will not be read, which means again the battle has been lost.

If, on the other hand, you are sending a resume to an individual and/or the decision-maker within an organization as a result of networking, there is a very good chance that your resume will be read with some care and attention. In this case, you may be competing with only a handful of other candidates — or the company might not even have a defined position for which they are hiring. (Yes, there are companies that will hire good people and then find a spot for them within the organization.)

Regardless of the circumstances surrounding the submission of a resume, a company always wants to know what you can do for them. As long as the skills and experiences on the resumes suggest that the candidates can all do the job, the one who will win is the one who can demonstrate the ability to actually make things happen. Are you beginning to see how those achievements you wrote in Chapter 1 might come into play?

You must be aware, at all times, that **your potential audience (even the OCR scanners used by large companies) will inevitably make assumptions and decisions, positive or negative, about you based on your resume** (ta da! a dirty secret). If the OCR (Optical Character Recognition) scanner does not find the key words for which it is searching, you will have lost the battle. Or if you have a Wharton MBA and are looking for a position with a small company, the assumption may be that you are too expensive, or will get bored, or will leave as soon as a Fortune 500 company calls. Or if you put a college graduation date of 1970 on your resume, you may be deemed to be too old (yes, I know that is discrimination, but try proving it).

Homework

Review the accomplishments you wrote for Chapter 1 to see how they might answer the potential employer's most crucial question: **"What can you do for me?"**

Once you have reviewed and further edited the accomplishments to focus on this question, group them into categories that might make sense for the types of positions you are after (categories might include sales, marketing, sales management, bottom-line results, leadership, team work, analysis, etc.). Keep in mind that some accomplishments could fall into more than one or two categories (for example, "led a sales team that increased revenue by 7 percent" is sales, team building, and leadership).

Chapter 3

Common Resume Pitfalls

Before we get into the specifics of resume writing, I think it might help to go over some of the more common problems that I have seen with resumes over the years. This list does not include sending in resumes that have little or nothing to do with the job that might be described in the advertisement. That is an entirely different discussion.

    A resume that is too long to be effectively scanned by a reviewer can be a large problem, as we discussed in earlier chapters. That is not to say that a two- or three-page resume is not appropriate, especially when you have given it directly to the decision-maker for a particular job opening. However, many job applicants include information such as hobbies, marital status, relocation preferences, every half-day educational seminar they have attended, every software application with which they have worked, and other data that are either extraneous or more appropriate for the interview. **A resume, aside from stating skills and experience, must answer the question "What can you do for me?" and very little else.** As with most rules, this one has it exceptions. If you know that a company is very involved in the community or a particular cause, then you should certainly include your civic or cause involvement on your resume. If you can include that involvement in your list of accomplishments, so much the better. If your civic or social involvement is a critical part of your core make-up, you may also want to always have it on your resume. It is a personal choice, however, and unless you know that it can directly advance your job search, I would recommend that you leave it off. You can always bring it up in the interview.

Sometimes less is more (another dirty secret). I have seen resumes that include repetitive job descriptions and accomplishments, as well as long and detailed job descriptions with every minute duty spelled out. Most of that can be considered "puffery," and all of these are inappropriate. Unless you have a job title that is totally unfamiliar to your potential readers, you should be able to omit most of the information about what you did; a resume reader will assume from the job title what your duties were. Details about your job functions should be discussed in the interview. An exception might be if you had duties that significantly exceeded your job title. For example, if you held the title of bookkeeper but were functioning as a CFO (finding financing, or negotiating contracts, etc.), then by all means include a job description that discusses chiefly those additional duties.

I have also seen resumes that are so "bare bones" that there are no job titles or descriptions included. There is nothing on which to even make a preliminary judgment of the applicant's skills. Guess where those resumes wind up? You have to pique the interest of the reader. If you do not, they will just move on to the next one in the pile.

The next major pitfall is the inclusion of inappropriate information. For example, justifications for leaving positions (the assumption will be that you have just admitted

Common Resume Pitfalls

that you were fired for cause), rationalizations for a lack of experience (the assumption being that you know that you are not qualified for the position), and the inappropriate use of acronyms. Every industry has its own language and abbreviations, as do government and the military. With one exception, assume that your potential audience has no idea what those acronyms and "buzz words" mean, and avoid their use. The exception to this is if you are responding to an advertisement that uses acronyms and/or industry jargon; you will want to incorporate those into your resume somewhere, as there is a good chance that your resume will be scanned by OCR (Optical Character Recognition) software for them.

Let's add to these pitfalls the inclusion of appropriate information that might be inappropriately framed. For example, your resume should include your email address; however, "cutesy" email addresses like hotstud@gmail.com or sweetiepie@aol.com do not convey a professional image and can easily cause you to be eliminated. Similarly, if you include a link to a Facebook or My Space page, make sure those pages are designed to present a professional image. Your friends might want to see you in a bathing suit chugging a beer; potential employers do not.

The last major pitfall is the use of self-limiting verbiage that might reduce your value or mitigate your experience. For example, in reviewing the resume for a young environmental engineer, just one year out of a very well-respected university, I noted that he had stated that he was looking for an entry-level engineering position. As I read the rest of the resume, the young man went on to describe two positions that he had held with engineering firms near the university. The applicant had work experience! Granted, the positions were internships, which he mentally discounted; hence the "entry level" designation. He may well have been correct in his assumption, but by including it in his resume, he unintentionally took himself out of the running for anything other than an entry-level position. Let the reader assume from the details that you are or are not qualified for a particular level of position.

Homework

Pull out any old resumes that you have for prior job searches or submissions, and review them for any of the errors described in this chapter. Highlight all the errors that you find, and keep the marked up resume for reference purposes as you write your new resume.

Set up professional email accounts and, if you want to refer to them, web pages that convey the image that you want the potential employer to have. Follow all the links you have provided to insure they do not lead to a site or page that is not appropriate for your job search.

Google yourself and check out the results. If your security settings on your My Space page are too lax, potential employers may access pictures and friends' comments that will work against you.

Chapter 4

Types of Resumes

There are an almost infinite number of resume formats. These formats are as varied as the individuals that write them. I talked with Beth Colley, a Certified Expert Resume Writer about this. Beth indicated that resumes can be put in three broad categories: chronological, functional, and combination. One general rule is that your name should always be the first item on the page. OCR programs typically store resumes by the first words they encounter, and you want that to be your name. You should also place your name first on every subsequent page of your resume.

The standard chronological resume has an executive summary (ES), written in the third person, that briefly captures the essential skills of the applicant. It might also include the type of position for which you are looking. The ES is a good place to highlight what you bring to the table (for example, "An experienced leader with a strong background in..."). Following the ES is a listing of each company for which you have worked, from the most recent backwards to the first job (you need not go back more than 10 years or so). Usually, this is where you will describe your job duties, major responsibilities, and accomplishments for each company. Following that will be the education and training section, which lists schools

So, Do You Want a Job, or What?

and dates attended as well as any degrees earned, again in reverse chronological order. (NOTE: if you attended a noteworthy institution, such as Harvard, Yale, MIT, or a military academy, you may want to put the education section before the job history for better visibility.) Some people will also list any significant training they have had. The final piece is what I call the miscellaneous section, where one might list significant social; fraternal, and/or civic activities (and some companies want to know about these items). Anyone who has five or more years of experience and three or more employers will have a resume of two to three pages.

If you are "of a certain age," you can omit some or all dates from your resume to further disguise your age. You will be questioned on this by resume reviewers. If you only list 10 years of your job history, including dates is a non-issue. You should avoid putting your graduation year in your education section, again to avoid assumptions about your age.

The advantages of a chronological resume are that it clearly shows continuous employment and steady advancement in an easy-to-follow format (which resume readers like). If, on the other hand, your employment history does not lend itself to a continuous orderly flow of jobs and advancement, or if you have jumped disciplines (perhaps gone from operations to sales to finance), those disconnects will be painfully obvious, which brings us to the functional resume.

A functional resume starts with the same executive summary. After the ES come functional achievements, which can be grouped in whatever areas you choose (leadership, sales, marketing, finance, operations, team building, etc.). Typically, the functional resume does not also include a job history section, although you may want to give it if there is room, followed by the same education, training, and miscellaneous sections.

The functional format is excellent for displaying a breadth of experience, and the functional areas can be re-ordered to emphasize a particular function for which the potential employer is looking. It is also an excellent way to emphasize all the intangibles that will grab the reader's attention. On the down side, it is more difficult to read and can cause the screener to assume that you are trying to hide something, especially if dates are omitted.

The last format is one that I believe is the strongest of the three: the combination (or as I like to structure it, the achievement) resume. In this format, the executive summary/job objective is similar to the other two formats. It is the second section that sets it apart. This section is the selective accomplishments section, and it consists of five to seven bullet points that detail what you have accomplished for other companies (as opposed to a listing of the duties associated with a job title). This should sound very familiar to you from your homework assignments in Chapters 1 and 2. You can customize the resume by picking the various achievements from your list that most closely match your understanding of the needs of the potential employer. The remainder of the resume can stay the same and follow the exact same format as the chronological or functional resume.

The great advantage of this format is that the critical information about your skills, capabilities, and results (what you bring to the table) appears in the top half of the first page in the ES and accomplishment sections, which is easily read in the 15-second window the reviewer might give the resume. The reviewer does not have to go to page

So, Do You Want a Job, or What?

two or three to find something that might grab him or her. If the achievement statements are powerful enough, there is no real need to even read the rest of the resume. By combining the achievements with either of the other two formats, you can take advantage of whichever format meets your needs while effectively communicating the critical intangible skills for which the potential employer is looking.

On the next page is a sample of this format.

Note: Turn to the Appendix 1, pages 68-71, to see my resume in the combination and one-page accomplishment formats.

Homework

You now have the elements and achievements written that will allow you to construct a solid resume that can attract favorable attention from potential employers. Using the one-page resume format opposite, develop your own one-page resume. After completing this exercise, put it away for a day or two, then review and edit it. Keep in mind that you are writing this for the potential employer; it must answer that important question "What can you do for me?"

After you believe it is complete and edited to your satisfaction, share it with your family and/or friends and ask them if they believe it reflects "you." Continue to repeat this process until everyone is satisfied with the result.

Sample One-Page Accomplishment Resume Format

Name (always the first item on a resume) **Address** (optional)
Phone Number **Email**
Website

Executive Summary/Job Objective: *Modify to mirror ad or employer perceived needs. This should be three to five sentences that describe your skills, strong intangibles, and the type of position for which you are looking. You might also add a very brief reason why you are going for that position, if it is different from your past experience. For example: A seasoned marketing executive, with a strong background in...is seeking an opportunity with a small business where I can truly make a positive impact on bottom line results.*

Selective Accomplishments: *Modify to mirror ad or employer perceived needs. Six to ten bullet points from your sorted accomplishments list that highlight the types of skills and intangibles for which you think the potential employer is looking.*

Employment History: *Listed chronologically or functionally, with or without dates.*

Education & Training: *List highest educational institution attended, degrees earned, and training THAT ADDS SIGNIFICANT VALUE to your background*

Miscellaneous *(add social, fraternal, civic or other PERTINENT information)*

So, Do You Want a Job, or What?

Congratulations, you now have a solid and "tight" resume. From this point on, you should develop a more detailed two- or three-page resume by adding accomplishments to the appropriate employer in the Employment History section and adding other miscellaneous items that you feel are appropriate. This version may be used for networking contacts where there is little or no competition for a position and a good chance that the reader will give it the due consideration you would like.

If you are looking at more than one major job discipline (for example, sales and operations), you may want to develop a one- and multi-page version for each major discipline.

Part 2

Dirty Secrets of Job Hunting

Chapter 5

Organizing Your Search Campaign

At this point, you have a valuable product to sell (yourself), and you understand the benefits that you bring to the table in an employment situation. Congratulations; you have just been promoted to the CEO position of the "Your Name Here" Marketing Company, Inc., and **your full-time job is to sell your product** (another dirty secret). So how do you go about doing that?

To start, you need to understand that 80 percent of all jobs are obtained through networking. This is not a dirty secret, but it is often ignored in the age of social networking via the Internet. **Many of those jobs are never advertised** (another dirty secret), and some do not even exist until the candidate appears with a solution to a problem that a company did not even know it had. I have had seven employers in my varied career, only two of which were obtained by responding to a published advertisement.

Many people sit behind their computers and blanket the world with resumes. They think they are being proactive and productive, but they are ignoring the bulk of the job marketplace. Not surprisingly, they send out hundreds of resumes with little or no response. To be effective at your job search, you should spend only 20 to 30 percent of your time responding to ads and registering yourself on company websites.

The bulk of your time should be spent networking. That is easy to say and hard to do, so let's start our discussion by talking about "prospecting." Prospecting is defined as — ***locating individuals ("suspects") within your target market, who you think might have information and/or contacts that will help you move your job search forward.*** If a suspect knows of an appropriate job opening and has the authority to hire for that position, the suspect then becomes a "prospect."

Until you are sure that you are meeting with a prospect, you should focus on seeking information (dirty secret time) on the company, industry, or direction of your search. A good technique to use while networking this way is to have business cards printed with your contact information on the front and your Executive Summary (from your resume) on the back. When you give out those cards, you provide convenient information that suspects can use to help you with your search.

While networking, do not tell people that you want to meet with them about a job. If you do, you have already started the sales process and most people will resist or dismiss you outright. You are seeking information on the industry and company, no more and no less. Your goal is to determine what the industry and/or company is going through and to get the names of other possible suspects with whom you can talk. Ideally, you will get the suspect with whom you are talking to "grease the skids" by calling referral contacts and introducing you. Do not be afraid to ask for these referrals and introductions. That is the purpose of your meeting.

Organizing Your Search Campaign

So how do you set up a meeting with a suspect? Start by generating a list of friends, acquaintances, or individuals in your target industry who fit the definition of a suspect. There are a lot of resources on the Internet, as well as various social networking sites that have this type of information; LinkedIn is a professional networking site that is specifically designed for this type of networking. You can also research your college alumni organizations and professional organizations (manufacturing associations, HR professional organizations, etc.) to which companies in your target markets belong. Your local library can be a great resource for you in developing your Suspect List.

Most people will be happy to advise or help you, if you only ask (making sure you are asking for information rather than a job). Once you have the list, start contacting these people to set up appointments. As you meet and network with these people, you will build and expand your network by asking for referrals (remember, you are focusing on getting information). The networking process takes time, but it is the best way to find a prospect. I once met with a job hunter in just such a circumstance. We had a nice conversation, and he left me his resume, while I gave him two referrals. A week later, a company with which I was working asked if I knew anyone with XYZ qualifications. I was happy to refer this person, and I got the added bonus of helping this company. Networking is all about relationships!

So let's see how effective networking works. Let's assume that you have developed a personal list of 20 people (family, friends and acquaintances, etc.); you call these people and make appointments with half of them. At each appointment, you get two referrals for other suspects, so you add 20 more people to your list. Because you have gotten "warm" referrals (remember that you have asked the referrer to grease the skids for you), you get 15 more appointments. Again, each appointment yields two additional referrals. In three to four rounds of this cycle, you will have networked your way into meeting 75 or more people who can and have helped you with your search. Pretty powerful stuff!

Networking Schematic

20 initial people on your list should yield 10 appointments. If each appointment averages 2 warm referrals, of which 3/4 will turn into appointments, after three rounds you will have had 45 appointments with suspects who might move your job search forward significantly.	20 Initial people on list ↓ 10 Initial interviews ↓ 20 Warm referrals ↓ 15 Secondary interviews ↓ 30 Warm referrals ↓ 20 Tertiary interviews ↓ 40 Warm referrals

If your search is a bit more modest (perhaps you are after an hourly type position), you may have to rely more on friends to tell you who is hiring, or you may want to go to the company in person to ask if they are hiring (or if they know someone else who is). Leave your resume and/or application. By making the effort to have a person-to-person contact, you have established an emotional bond (dirty secret!). You are no longer one resume in a pile, but a real live human being, which might give you a slight advantage; taking the time to go there in person demonstrates your interest as well.

Homework

Make a list of 20 to 30 people who you would consider suspects. Start with family and friends, and expand from there. As you network through these people, expand your list with the referrals you have gotten in your meetings with various suspects. Practice interviewing with friends who can give you honest feedback on how you did.

Do not throw this list away. This is the beginning of your network, which you can use again and again — not only for job hunting, but also in the day-to-day performance of your new job. In the networking world, contacts are gold; stay in touch with them on a periodic basis. **Your network can move you forward in ways you cannot even imagine** (a powerful dirty secret).

Chapter 6

Goal-Setting and Metrics

Activity will equal results in your job-hunting campaign. The more you network and the more appointments you have, the faster you will get the results for which you are looking (A JOB!). For most of us working alone at home, it is difficult to stay focused and motivated throughout the process. One way that I have found that helps me to stay focused is to set written goals and establish metrics, so that I can **objectively measure my activity and results on a daily basis** (dirty secret yet again).

Let's start with the goal-setting process. I am using the goal-setting process developed and copyrighted by Resource Associates Corporation (RAC), as it is the most effective and logical process I have ever come across for goal setting (I refer to their methodology with permission). In order for a goal to be effectively used, it must be a WHYSMART goal; WHYSMART stands for **Written, Harmonious, Yours, Specific, Measurable, Achievable, Realistically high, and Time sensitive**.

If a goal is important enough to set, you must put it in **writing**. If you do not, in the day-to-day hustle and bustle, you will lose track of it only to realize weeks later that you forgot about the goal that you so wanted to achieve. It must be **harmonious** — that is to say, it must be compatible with other goals and demands that you are currently facing. It also has to be **your goal**. The reason we fail to keep most of our New Year's resolutions is that they are usually goals that we have set because others want that result for us. If you are not doing it for yourself, there is little chance that you will achieve it. Your goal must be **specific**, and it must be **measurable**; otherwise, how will you know when you have achieved it? A goal must be both **achievable** and **realistically high**; if you do not have to stretch to attain it, what is the point in having the goal? At the same time, you need to insure that the goal is within the realm of reality, or you are just setting yourself up for failure. Finally, a goal must be **time sensitive**. If you set a specific date for reaching the goal, you will develop both a sense of urgency for gaining it and a trigger mechanism for you to evaluate your results.

Now we can discuss what to do after you have written down your WHYSMART goals. For each goal you have developed (and there may be multiple goals that apply to your job-hunting efforts), identify every single obstacle that you can think of that might prevent you from reaching that goal. One major obstacle that most of us tend to overlook is ourselves. As Pogo used to say (those of us who are of a certain age will remember), "We have seen the enemy, and he is us!" Recognize that **your natural reluctance to do unfamiliar things and change your habits is a major obstacle to overcome** (a huge dirty secret). You will find that you must force yourself to do these uncomfortable tasks every day. The good news is that over time the tasks will become easier to do, until you wake up one morning to find that they have become new and productive habits that you do without conscious effort.

Next, consider what the rewards might be for achieving the goal — and what the consequences might be for not achieving the goal. Weighing the rewards and consequences will tell you if the goal is appropriate and worthwhile. Assuming that the goals you have set for your job search are worthwhile, the next step is to identify a solution for every single obstacle that you have previously identified.

Once the solutions have been identified, you will need to develop action steps for implementing them. Each step in your action plan should have a due date associated with it, and the due dates must predate or correspond to the date you set for achieving the goal. Keep in mind that all of this should be put in writing and posted prominently in your office or work space. You should be reviewing these plans on a routine basis to insure that you are on track with achieving the goals and objectives.

If you miss a deadline for achieving a goal, do not beat yourself up over it. Rather, examine why you missed it. What obstacle did you not identify, or what action step(s) did you miss? When you have figure out what went wrong, you can reset and try again.

A RAC affiliate once told me about a measurement system that she used to track her daily productivity. It involved scoring points for various daily activities and striving to obtain a daily minimum acceptable total score. I have adapted it to the job-hunting arena and offer it here for your consideration:

So, Do You Want a Job, or What?

Task	Points
Sending out a resume	0.25
Talking to a live suspect on the phone	1
Setting up a networking appointment	2
Going to a networking appointment	3
Going to a job interview	4

The daily goal is to amass four points each and every day, five days a week. Your daily job-search work cannot be considered complete until you achieve your minimum four points every day. You can track yourself by writing your daily score on your calendar. If you are routinely getting your four points but are not moving your job search forward as fast as you would like, change the minimum daily score to six or eight points. In other words, set the bar higher (remember Achievable and Realistically High?). If you are not hitting your four points a day, take a hard look at what is stopping you. Once you have identified the obstacle, develop a new action plan to overcome the new obstacle.

Homework

Develop goals for your new company, "Your Name Here" Marketing, Inc. Start by developing goal categories. Write down all the goal areas that you think are important for your success. Put the list away for a day or two, and then take it out and review it in detail. When you are satisfied that you have captured everything that is important, share the list with a friend or colleague for independent verification.

With the goal categories developed, take each one and develop it into a WHYSMART goal. For each WHYSMART

Goal-Setting and Metrics

goal, go through the complete goal-setting process by identifying obstacles, rewards, consequences, solutions, etc., until you have a detailed action plan for each goal and, therefore, for your search overall. Put all of this in writing and prominently post it in your work area. You will need to review it routinely.

Order "business" cards with your contact information on the front and your Executive Summary on the back. **Hand these out at networking functions or wherever you feel comfortable doing so. It will set you apart from the crowd** (an important dirty secret).

Chapter 7

Maintaining a Positive Attitude

Perhaps the toughest part of the job search effort is to hold on to the positive attitude that is vital for maintaining the activity level necessary to achieve your goal of getting a new job. It is very difficult for most people to work in a vacuum without a lot of feedback and still keep their positive attitude and focus. We are social creatures and need human interaction to reinforce that we are valued human beings. Without that feedback, we can easily convince ourselves that we are alone in our predicament, and that no one cares about us.

On the back of my business cards, I have printed a formula, developed by Resource Associates Corporation (RAC), that captures the central role attitude plays. It reads:

$$ASK + Goals = PBC \Rightarrow IR \;^{\copyright RAC}$$

Attitude, Skills, and Knowledge plus (written) Goals equal Positive Behavioral Change, which yields Improved Results. Translated, that means you can have all the skills and knowledge to do a task, but if your attitude is lacking, the task will not get done. So how do you develop the right attitude for a job search? **You must strike a balance in**

your life in the midst of the turmoil of a job search (a vital dirty secret).

Start with the physical side of the equation. A job search is stressful. One of the best ways to combat stress is to exercise regularly. Go out every morning or evening for a 30-minute walk, or go to the gym, or ride a bike. Just do it regularly, on a schedule.

Because you have the free time, you might be tempted to stay up late or sleep in every morning. Resist that urge. Job hunting is a full-time job, and to be effective you need to establish a regular schedule. Maybe you'll check websites and send out resumes in the morning, make your networking calls mid-morning, and schedule appointments for lunch or for the afternoon. It does not matter what the routine is; it just matters that you have a routine.

Having a routine accomplishes three things. First, it helps you mimic the daily work routine just like you would have for any job. Second, having a routine makes life somewhat less stressful. Finally a routine makes it more likely that you will get to sleep at a reasonable hour, which is another great stress reducer.

Keep up your spiritual activities, as well. If you are religious, make sure you continue to attend services. You might want to volunteer more within your faith-based institution(s). You will draw moral support from these (and it is also a good networking activity), and volunteering will enhance your sense of self-worth. If you are not religious, get involved with your community, youth activities, and/or social groups for exactly the same reasons. It is important to interact with others in activities that are not pure networking opportunities, although any group interaction is always a networking opportunity (so always carry your business cards with you). Having a purpose matters.

Stay involved with your family. They can be a natural support group for you, if you allow them to help. We tend to draw away from family and friends because we feel awkward or embarrassed during the job search, and we want to spare them the added stress of our situation. The reality is that drawing away increases stress on those around us and increases our own stress even further. Similarly, stay in touch with your friends and former colleagues. They can be a good source of support as well as possible leads for your job search.

With the loss of your former income, you might consider getting outside advice on money management issues. Many financial advisors will be willing to talk with you about these issues without charging you any fee at all. Keeping a handle on your expenses will also help to reduce stress.

Look for employment support groups, and, if there are none, consider starting one. Support groups can keep you focused on the task at hand and are a way for you to get and give feedback on your activities. You might also want to look for a mentor or coach with whom you can touch base routinely to discuss what you are doing and to get more feedback on what is and is not working for you. Having some level of external support is a crucial piece of the puzzle for maintaining a positive attitude.

Homework

Develop a daily schedule for yourself that includes exercise, work activities, volunteer time, and family time.

Search for volunteering opportunities with your faith-based organization and/or local schools, non-profits, and civic organizations. One word of caution: Don't let these activities take up more time than you can afford from your new work schedule for your job search.

Chapter 8

Entrepreneurship and Independent Income Streams

If you have always wanted to be your own boss, you might now find yourself in a position to take a shot at starting up your own business. Or, perhaps you have been in the job-search mode for a number of months and are starting to get nervous about your financial situation. I fully sympathize with both scenarios, due mainly to the fact that I have been in both of them. There are a number of opportunities out there that you might want to take advantage of, but you need to be careful and very selective with them. **When our needs are great enough, we tend to only see the possibilities and ignore the risks** (a dirty secret).

Let's talk first about starting your own company. You may have a good or even a great concept for a start-up business; however, a concept does not a business make. Lots of people who love to cook, for example, dream of starting a restaurant. This requires money — lots of money. It also takes lots of work, especially in areas in which the amateur chef may not have any expertise. Can you negotiate a lease, or manage a staff, or create effective advertising, or manage the accounting, or cope with very long days? Granted, there are many professionals out there who can assist you with

So, Do You Want a Job, or What?

all those tasks for a fee, and there are even more people out there who claim that they can assist you, again for a fee, but who do not have the requisite skills for doing so.

If you are going to start your own business, you must first have a complete and solid business plan that addresses all those concerns. You also need a pro forma profit-and-loss statement and cash-flow projections, based on reasonable assumptions that will indicate the total level of investment that you will need to get the business to a self-sustaining level of profitability. Again, there are professionals who can assist you with this essential preliminary planning. Interview a number of small business accountants and CPAs who have experience in the industry in which you are interested. There are also business attorneys, business consultants, and coaches who also have the experience to help you. To sort the wheat from the chaff, talk with a number of these sources and check their references. Whatever else you do, do not try to go it alone.

I get at least four emails every week from companies that are trying to sell franchise opportunities, and that may be a legitimate way to go. **However, if you think that a franchise is a simple and foolproof way to get into business for yourself, please think again** (a very dirty secret). I have worked with two franchise owners whose businesses failed due to a lack of support from the franchisor. Not all franchises are created equal. Some provide "soup to nuts" support; others do not. You must do your homework on these opportunities and, again, talk to a number of business professionals before you invest.

One franchisee with whom I worked was talked into using virtually every penny he had to start up the franchise. The franchisor implied that lenders would be more than willing to help him, should he ever need it, just due to the fact that he had invested his own money (demonstrating his total commitment to the venture). But the truth is that lenders need both a solid business plan and collateral in order to agree to lend money. The franchisee found out too late that he was so leveraged that he could not qualify for the operating capital line of credit he needed to fund the business for the one to two years it would take to get past breakeven to profitability. He eventually closed the business and was forced to file for bankruptcy. Remember that for every business success story, there are six horror stories of business failures. I am not suggesting that franchises are bad, but some outfits provide more help and support than others. Nevertheless, the franchisors have their own agenda and goals, which probably do not coincide with yours.

I also get four or five emails a day touting work-at-home Internet opportunities, some of which are legitimate. There are also a large number of Multi-Level Marketing (MLM) companies that push sales of products directly to the end user, bypassing retail outlets. Many of these are indeed good opportunities for the right person. Typically, the products are good, and sometimes the products are even far superior to others on the market. **The devil, as always, is in the details.** Do these MLM opportunities require you to buy lots of inventory, which you then turn around and sell? If so, be careful. Is your new function to recruit others to the cause? If so, be careful. Will you be required to set-up and lead "product" parties to both sell product and recruit new members? If so, does that fit your personality?

It is not that these opportunities are not legitimate; they are...for the right person. If you are an outgoing, enthusiastic, rah-rah type of person, then one of these might be right for you. It has been my experience, however, that most people do not fit that mold. With all these MLM companies, you need to investigate and evaluate how the company functions and what will be asked of you. If you cannot "sell," most of these opportunities are not for you. If, however, you want a little extra money, these options might be just what the doctor ordered. But do not be fooled by promises of easy and fast money; anything that pays well requires hard work. Take the time to talk with friends and business professionals before you jump into any of these. Aside from the wildly inflated promises, with which many of us become disillusioned, diverting significant amounts of your energy into these will only take away from your job-search efforts, which might cause you to miss opportunity when she does knock.

Homework

(This only applies if you fall into the entrepreneurial or business start-up/ MLM realm.)

Look before you leap. If an idea sounds too good to be true, it probably is! That being said, do massive research on any option at which you are looking. You can find lots of information online about business start-ups, franchises, and MLM opportunities. While the information is not vetted, it can raise some flags that must be checked out before proceeding.

For business start-ups, ask yourself this one overriding question before proceeding:

> ***"Why should anyone buy (insert your product or service here), and especially from me?"***

If you cannot answer this convincingly for yourself, your family, and friends, take a long hard look at the opportunity before proceeding. The answer to that question will frame your marketing and sales effort for your business. Without a marketing and sales plan, even the greatest idea will not fly!

If you are looking at a franchise, at least find out the answers to these questions during your research and due diligence efforts:

> ▹ What is the failure rate of new franchises?
> ▹ What detailed assistance does the franchisor contractually commit to giving?
> ▹ What are the financing options, and will the franchisor help with finding start-up cash?
> ▹ What kind of marketing and sales training is offered?
> ▹ Are there defined territories, and how are they set up?

For MLM opportunities, you might want to ask these types of questions:

> ▹ How are the products sold?
> ▹ How is prospecting for customers done?
> ▹ What is my total investment going to be?
> ▹ How long does it take an average person to reach [insert your monetary goal here]?
> ▹ What is the typical closing rate on sales?
> ▹ Does this opportunity fit my personality and skill sets?

Chapter 9

Selling Yourself

Another big step forward: You have an interview! Now you begin the sales process, because **job hunting is a sales process** (a vital dirty secret), and you need to understand the basic fundamentals of that process. I will be using the Resource Associates Corporation's sales process (with permission), since it is the one with which I am most familiar, and it gets down to the nitty-gritty quickly.

The sales process is a six-step process. The first two steps are *Introduction* and *Gaining Favorable Attention*. Almost invariably, people hire/buy on an emotional basis and justify the decision with facts and logic afterward. For job hunting, steps one and two begin with your networking and resume, via which you establish first impressions and the emotional bonds that will drive the hiring decision later. It is important to carry out these steps so that you continue to gain favorable attention throughout the entire hiring process. With every different interviewer, you must establish a positive first impression so that you can continue to receive favorable attention with that person; both you and the prospect need to be comfortable with each other. For example, I found out after the fact that the Operations Manager at Procter & Gamble decided to hire me three minutes into the initial interview. Even though

So, Do You Want a Job, or What?

I spent six hours interviewing with three other managers, any one of whom could have vetoed that hiring decision, the decision was made based on my resume and the first impression I made on the Operations Manager.

Do not try to pretend you are something you are not. You cannot "fake" your way through an interview. If you have done your homework from Part I of this book, you will know and be comfortable talking about you. Faking intangible qualities will almost always come across as insincere. Be confident, self-assured, and yourself.

Step three is *Discovering Wants and Needs*. **People buy products for the benefit the product provides** (a dirty secret). You do not buy clothes to cover your naked body and protect you from the elements. You buy clothes that make you look and feel good while achieving those utilitarian goals. Similarly, companies hire people not just for their skills and knowledge but also because they think that the person they are hiring will provide the benefit(s) for which they are looking. That is, the company thinks the people will do the job while fitting into the company culture and, possibly, do the job better, faster, easier, or cheaper. To that end, you need to find out during the interviewing process what skill sets are needed for the position and what the intangible qualities the company needs to fill for the position. Translated, that means you ask lots of pertinent questions and listen carefully for the answers. Let the interviewer do the bulk of the talking. Here are a few sample questions, you might want to consider:

- Why is this position available?
- Can you describe the company's management philosophy?

> What would be the first three things you would want your new employee to address?
> How does the company manage change?
> How would you measure performance in this position?

The goal is to understand, in detail, what the company is looking for in terms of skills as well as the intangibles that you would bring to the table. When you are sure you fully understand the wants and needs, ask another question, just to make sure. **If you jump the gun and start offering solutions without knowing the real issues, you can talk your way right out of a position** (a dirty secret).

Step four is to *Present Benefits and Consequences*. Once you truly understand the company's wants and needs, you can determine how you represent the solution to them. This is where all that resume work on your accomplishments comes into play. You have thought through, understand, and can easily articulate how you can provide the benefits for which the company is looking. This is the heart of the selling process. If you jump to this step too soon, however, you will lose the sale!

Most people go through a variety of levels of interviewing. Keep in mind that most of the people with whom you interview will have input into the decision, but only one will have the full responsibility for the decision. Even if the hiring is done by committee, there is always one person who controls the process. This person is the prospect and is the one step four is designed to impress. You need to go through the process with all the interviewers, but the prospect is the one you really want to sell.

Step five is *Getting Commitment*. If you have done your job well up to this point, getting a commitment should be a natural progression of the process; however, the company will probably want to do some deliberations, and possibly more interviews, before making a final decision. First, you want to formally express your interest and ask for the job! If you do not ask for the job, the interviewer(s) may assume that you are less than enthusiastic. Then find out the timing for the decision-making process.

The final step is *Follow-up*. Sending thank you notes to everyone who interviewed you and calling promptly on the follow-up date are critically important. No matter what was said or implied in the interviews, nothing is guaranteed. This should be viewed not as the end of the process but as the start of a new long-term process between you and the company.

Homework

Before you actually go for an interview with a company, do your homework. Research the company online. Find out everything you can about the company, its products, and its management. Do a Google search of the company. Also check with that wonderful network you have so carefully built during your job search. Find people from that or similar companies, and talk to them about the company with which you are getting ready to interview. Try to understand their strengths and weaknesses. More importantly, try to get an idea of what their current challenges might be. If you are prepared to talk about the company intelligently, you will be head and shoulders above your competition.

Know where you are going for the interview. Do not assume that because you know the general area that you will know where it is located. If necessary, drive to the location a day or two ahead so that you will be sure to arrive early.

Dress appropriately. It is better to be over-dressed than to be dressed more casually than the interviewer.

After the interview, send personal handwritten thank you notes to everyone with whom you talked. Gaining favorable attention does not stop when you leave after the interview!

Finally, if you have accepted the position, you have to let everyone with whom you talked in your networking efforts know that you are now gainfully employed and thank them for their assistance with your search. **Do not forget about your network** (a long-term, and my last dirty secret); you have expended a lot of time and energy building it. Continue to stay in touch with these people periodically for two reasons. First, they might be very helpful to you in your current position, and you might actually be able to help them should they find themselves in your previous predicament. Second, you never know when you might again be on the outside looking in and again be in need of that network.

Appendix

Sample Resumes

So, Do You Want a Job, or What?

Original Resume

JOHN L. NICODEMUS

OPERATIONS EXECUTIVE WITH BOTTOM LINE ACCOUNTABILITY

Leadership...Production Management...Profit Improvement...Revitalization...Strategic Planning...Product/Process Development...P&L Management...Cash Flow Management...Building High Performance Teams...Service Industry Experience...Customer Satisfaction...Materials Management...Regulatory Management Experience...Inventory Reduction...Engineering Supervision...

PROFILE

An efficient and resourceful senior manager, I am capable of achieving true profitability through enhancing real time performance in industrial technology. In an operational leadership role, I will motivate people to drive change across all levels of the organization while maximizing employee performance. My creative managerial style as a high-energy performer is best defined by my ability to find opportunities that will foster continuous improvement, with outstanding customer satisfaction and ultimately provide top-notch profitability.

EXPERIENCE AND ACCOMPLISHMENTS

2003 – PRESENT **JLN ASSOCIATES INC.**
A privately held group focused on operational management consulting with an emphasis on cash flow management and turn around, workout and crisis management consulting.
CEO
Full accountability for the total operation of the organization, from prospecting new clients to final delivery.

♦ Revitalized a manufacturer of specialized automotive aftermarket components, including valuation of the company. Developed a simple cash flow system and reworked infrastructure to successfully convert the company from a part-time hobby to a full time business.

♦ Utilized the 13-week cash flow format to focus management on both deficiencies within the organization and critically important issues, defining the size of their monetary short fall and helping them to focus and establish strategic partnerships that would return the company to profitability.

Appendix

1990 – 2003 EXECUTIVE SOUNDING BOARD ASSOCIATES, INC.
A turn around workout and crisis management consulting firm.
2002 – 2003 Director
Managed clients from initial sales call through the final deliverables.
♦ Set a new management precedent while advising an insulation supplier to the commercial construction industry, by flowcharting and then streamlining their order processing, achieving a 500% improvement in order processing time, identifying and eliminating bottlenecks, while adding ERP computerization and necessary management to improve productivity and profitability.

1990 – 2000 Managing Director
Accountable for the marketing direction of the Baltimore office, and establish policies and procedures for the firm as well as managing clients through the final deliverables.
♦ Crisis managed a rapidly failing $120 million dollar manufacturing company, operating at a -8% gross margin, assumed control of the operation, tripled production, reduced quality defects by 90%, reduced staffing by 50% and implemented more than $5 million dollars in annualized cost savings. The company's gross margin grew to 24%, returning it to solid profitability.

2000 – 2002 PROFESSIONAL ENVIRONMENTAL MANAGEMENT ENTERPRISES, INC.
A $6 million dollar, 500 employee, commercial janitorial firm.
CEO
Responsible for day-to-day management, sales, marketing, profitability, and both customer development and service for the company.
♦ Neutralized an employee walkout that occurred just prior to my start, by hiring temporary management from an out-of-state firm, identifying and promoting high performing employees to management positions and recruiting several new managers from outside of the organization with no disruption in services.

1988 –1990 GENERAL MAINTENANCE SERVICE COMPANY
A $14 million dollar, 1600 employee, commercial janitorial firm.
Operations Manager
Managed 100 different accounts both the day-to-day operations as well as their bottom line profitability. My scope of responsibility included 800 employees.
♦ Developed a program to hire an untapped source for employees' specifically "homeless" individuals, improving overall morale, reduced employee turnover by at least 5% and saved the company $25,000 per year in employee training costs.

So, Do You Want a Job, or What?

1984 – 1988 **KAMAR SERVICES INC.**
A $3 million dollar, 25 employee, warehousing and distribution company.
Vice President and General Manager
Responsible for all internal operations of the company.
♦ Improved the pick-pack process by developing a system to hire from the ranks of the mentally challenged, resulting in a 15% process improvement that saved the company $10,000 per year in reshipping costs.
♦ Developed product changeover procedures reducing the time from several hours to a minimum of 15 minutes, saving approximately $15,000 in overtime.

1978 – 1984 **PROCTER & GAMBLE**
1980 – 1984 **Manager Professional and Regulatory Services**
Accountable for ensuring full compliance with FDA regulation for a line of disposable surgical drapes and gowns (Class II medical devices), as well as other paper products. Also accountable for the gamma sterilization process for the line of disposable surgical drapes and gowns.
♦ Problem-solved a health oriented, adverse employee reaction to a consumer product by examining all of the related processes and arriving at the definitive solution, without room for error.

EDUCATION

Bachelor of Science, Engineering
United States Military Academy, West Point, NY

Appendix

One-page Accomplishment Resume

JOHN L. NICODEMUS
www.linkedin/in/johnnicodemus   email –

Senior Executive with highly successful experience in improving performance for all facets of manufacturing, financial and business management for companies ranging in size from start-ups to Fortune 20.

- Led four different financially-troubled companies back to solid profitability by:
    o **Establishing** logical and efficient organizational structures
    o **Building** effective management teams
    o **Improving** manufacturing efficiencies to impact both top and bottom line results
    o **Optimizing** cash flow
- **Increased** production efficiency resulting in gains of 125% and a gross margin increase from -8% to 15%.
- **Directed** the shift of 90% of a Company's production offshore increasing the gross margin from 7% to 21%.
- **Reorganized** the operations staff of a non-profit company allowing it to pay down more than $5 mm of debt
- **Identified** and **corrected** quality defect in the formulation for an extrusion product, resulting in an immediate 80% improvement in quality resulting in a cost savings of $1.5 million.

BS in Engineering, United States Military Academy, West Point, New York

Professional Experience

Principal, JLN Associates, d/b/a Call The Man, Inc.

- Developed a cash flow forecasting tool resulting in a 40% improvement in collections days outstanding.
- Developed a strategic partnership for a company with a customer, which increased sales by 15% and gross margins 23%.
- Improved results through action-plan driven change facilitation

CEO, Professional Environmemental Management Entreprises, Inc.

- Reduced employee turnover from 30% to less than 10% eliminating more than $250k in new employee training costs.
- Developed a quality tracking system that improved performance and resulted in $500k in increased sales.

Director/Managing Director, Executive Sounding Board Associates, Inc.

- Led group of supervisors through cost-saving sessions resulting in more than $5 million in cost savings.
- Implemented an ERP software system at a manufacturing facility increasing gross margin by 20%.

Operations Manager, General Maintenance Service Company

- Managed P&L for $50mm in business consisting of 100 accounts and 1,500 full and part-time employees.
- Developed an approach to hiring which improved staffing levels and reduced turnover by 5% saving $25,000 per year.

VP and General Manager, KAMAR Services, Inc.

- Managed the start-up and grew a distribution company from $800k to $3 mm in sales in less than three years.
- Developed a pick-line design that reduced product changeovers from two hours to 15 minutes.

The Procter and Gamble Company
Manager Professional & Regulatory Affairs/ Quality Control Manager/Area Manager

- Managed the gamma radiation sterilization program for the *Boundary*® line of surgical drapes and gowns.
- Developed a new approach to leading production teams, which eliminated 3 managers saving $225k per year.

Publications

- "So, Do You Want A Job, Or What", to be published winter 2010
- "Operational Crisis Management", ***The Secured Lender***, March/April 1996, pg. 84
- "Manufacturing Systems: A Cautionary Tale", ***Corporate Renewal***, Vol.13/No.1, January 2000, pg. 12

About the Author

John Nicodemus is a 1973 graduate of the US Military Academy at West Point, NY. After spending five years in the military, John was hired by Procter & Gamble at their paper production plant in Albany, GA. While with Procter & Gamble, John moved to the Cellulose and Specialties Division in Memphis, TN and finally to Paper Division R&D Center in Cincinnati, Ohio.

After more than 15 years working within the military and a large corporation, John realized that he did not fit the large corporate model and focused his career on the small business model. As a partner in a boutique consulting firm specializing in working with troubled companies, John was directly involved in the hiring and firing decisions for a number of clients. Over the years, John reviewed hundreds of resumes and interviewed many potential candidates for a variety of positions.

John has also experienced unemployment personally and understands the issue from both perspectives.

Index

A
accomplishment resume — 13
accomplishments — 18, 20, 21, 25, 28, 31, 33, 35, 63
acronyms — 29
age — 32, 39, 46
alumni organizations — 41
audience — 23, 25, 29

B
business coach — 11
business plan — 56, 57
buzz words — 29

C
chronological resume — 31-33
civic — 28, 32, 35, 54
Colley, Beth — 31
combination resume — 31, 33, 34
confidence — 20
Covington, John — 7

D
degrees — 31, 35
dirty secret — 18, 19, 23-25, 28, 39, 40, 42, 43, 45, 46, 49, 52, 55, 56, 61-63, 65

E
education — 31-33
email address — 29
employment group — 11, 20
Entrepreneurship — 9, 55
ES. *See* executive summary
executive summary — 31-33
experience — 11, 17, 18, 24, 27, 29, 32, 33, 35, 36, 56, 58

F
Facebook — 29
feedback — 43, 51, 53
Findiesen, Rodger — 7
first impressions — 61
focus — 20, 25, 40, 51
franchise — 56, 59
franchisee — 56, 57
fraternal — 20, 32, 35
functional resume — 31-33

G
goal-setting — 45, 49
Google — 13, 30, 64
graduation year — 32

H

I
intangibles — 19, 20, 33, 35, 63
interview — 18-20, 27, 28, 48, 61-65

J
job-hunting process — 12
job duties — 31
job market — 11
job search strategy — 12
job seeker — 11, 12
job title — 28, 33

K

L
library — 41
LinkedIn — 41

Index

M
measurement system — 47
mentor — 11, 53
mentoring — 11, 12, 20
MLM — 57, 58, 59
Multi-Level Marketing. *See* MLM
My Space — 29, 30

N
network — 41, 43, 45, 64, 65
networking — 24, 36, 39, 40, 41, 43, 48, 49, 52, 61, 65
Networking Schematic — 42

O
obstacle — 46-48
OCR — 25, 29, 31
Optical Character Recognition. *See also* OCR
optical scanner — 23

P
Peduto, Mike — 20
pitfall — 28, 29
positive attitude — 51, 53
professional organizations — 41
prospects — 24
puffery — 19, 28

Q
qualified candidate — 24

R
Resource Associates Corporation — 45, 51, 61
responsibilities — 31
resume — 11, 13, 17-21, 23-25, 27-36, 40-42, 48, 61-63
risks — 55
routine — 47, 52

S

"suspects" — 40
schools — 31, 53
self-awareness — 20
sell yourself — 12
social — 20, 28, 32, 35, 39, 41, 51, 52
Stevton Consulting — 20
stress — 52, 53
support group — 12, 53

T

team leader — 19
thank you notes — 64, 65
tool — 12, 17, 18
training — 12, 31-33, 35, 59

U

V

W

What can you do for me? — 25, 27, 34
WHYSMART — 45, 46, 48
work history — 18

X

Y

Z